THE
SEVEN
DEADLY
SINS

THE
SEVEN
DEADLY
SINS HOW THEY
RIVAL GOD'S LOVE

J. McKinley Williams III

REDEMPTION ◆ PRESS

Published by Redemption Press, PO Box 427, Enumclaw, WA 98022

ISBN 13: 978-1-63232-259-3
Library of Congress Catalog Card Number: 2011917473

This book is dedicated
to the memory of my natural mother,
CeCelia D. Williams, 1937 - 1984
and in honor of my wife, Susan, and my three daughters,
CeCelia, Shelby, and Lillian

CONTENTS

ACKNOWLEDGMENTS

I STAND ON the shoulders of many giants who have helped me. I would like to thank them all. First, I would like to express my thanks to our Lord. Next, I would to thank my wife and soul mate, Susan, who encouraged me to go after the dream of writing this Bible study.

I would like thank my parents (my natural mother, Cecelia, my father, John Jr., and my mother, Ginny), for all of the sacrifices they made for me. I could not have completed my education without their help. I would like to thank my sisters, Teresa, Chris, and Becky, for their roles in helping me as their little brother. I would like to thank my college and seminary professors and former churches where I served as a pastor. I would also like to express appreciation to my peers in ministry with whom I have served.

INTRODUCTION

S IN SETS US apart from our relationship with God and each other. God created us to be in relationship with Himself. Just as sin created distance in the relationship that Adam and Eve had with God, sin creates distance in the relationship we have with God and in relationships with others. From the beginning of Genesis, God created a sinless world and everything in it. Adam and Eve's sin changed that.

One of the ways we can describe sin is rebellion. When we sin, we are rebelling against God's love. As the apostle Paul said, we have all sinned and have fallen short of the glory of God (see Rom. 3:23). If we needed an acronym for sin we could say that the "s" stands for *subtle*, the "i" stands for *invasive*, and the "n" stands for *nullifying*. Though sin's destruction may not always be immediate, it is still a destructive force.

Historically, the seven deadly sins (SDS) have been understood as "destructive" for centuries. They are destructive to individuals as well as to the community. Although there is no list of the SDS in the Bible, the destructive nature of them can be seen in various places throughout the Bible. The seven deadly sins rival God's love. "God saw everything he had made: it was supremely good" (Gen. 1:31 CEB). God even created humans in God's own image (see Gen. 1:27). Sin is therefore destructive to the camaraderie that God shares with humanity. It is also destructive to the peace, love, and goodwill God intended for us to have with our fellow human beings. For that reason, we can conclude that the seven deadly sins rival God's love.

CHAPTER 1
THE SIN OF PRIDE

Luke 18:11-14

God created the world out of nothing, and as long as we are nothing,
He can make something out of us.

—Martin Luther[1]

He who climbs too high is near a fall.

—Italian proverb[2]

Sincere humility attracts. Lack of humility subtracts. Artificial humility
detracts.

—Italian Proverb[3]

Humility is pride in God.

—Austin O'malley[4]

Nothing sets a person so much out of the devil's reach as humility.

—Jonathan Edwards[5]

Most people would succeed in small things if they were not troubled with great ambitions.
                                    —Henry Wadsworth Longfellow[6]

Humility is a strange thing: The moment you think you have it, you have lost it.
                                    —Anonymous[7]

Humility is not the belittling of self; it is the forgetting of self.
                                    —Anonymous[8]

There is no true holiness without humility.
                                    —Thomas Fuller, M. D., Gnomologia[9]

Soar not too high to fall; but stoop to rise.
                                    —Philip Massinger, The Duke of Milan, I.[10]

DURING THE 70s, popular music artist Carly Simon wrote a song entitled, "You're So Vain." It is said she wrote that song about Warren Beatty because he thought that he was God's gift to women. Some of the lyrics to that song go like this: "You're so vain, you probably think this song's about you."

According to Paul, vanity such as that comes when someone thinks more highly of himself/herself than he ought to think (see Rom. 12:3). James 4:6 says, "God opposes the proud but gives grace to the humble." Pride in its original God-given context is not a bad thing. The kind of pride God opposes is the kind that is arrogant and condescending. Racism, sexism, ageism, nationalism, denominationalism, subordination due to social class, intellectual conceit, and flaunting success through materialism are all forms of pride that are condescending. Egotism is at the root of all of them.

Looking at this parable, we will be able to see the way the Pharisee saw himself, God, and others.

2

THE WAY THE PHARISEE SAW HIMSELF

He Saw Himself as Above Reproach

According to the self-assessment of the Pharisee, he did no wrong in the eyes of God. He saw himself as the epitome of proper conduct. He fasted twice a week. He gave a tenth of all his income. He did all the right things, but for the wrong reasons. It seems that he did all that he did to get the praise of men. Consider what Matthew 6:5 says: "And when you pray, do not be like the hypocrites, for they love to pray standing in the synagogues and on the street corners to be seen by men." That is precisely what the Pharisee did when he went up to the temple to pray. He stood up (see Luke 18:11). There are two things we can gather from the Pharisee's sanctimonious attitude. First, the fact that he stood up is an indication that he saw himself above reproach as he physically exalted himself. Second, he looked down on everyone else who was not just like him.

He Looked Down on Others with an Attitude of Scorn

To be scornful of someone is to look at him/her with shame, disgust, and disappointment. Pharisees were not good at looking at themselves in the mirror. They were good at pointing out the flaws of others while they neglected to see their own. When we do that, we tend to treat others based upon how we have judged them, rather than treating them as equals.

It is said that Dorothy Parker once attended a social gathering. In the group was a celebrity who was vain and proud. During the conversation the celebrity declared condescendingly, "I always try to be gracious to my inferiors." "How wonderful," purred the disarming Parker. "But tell me, where do you find them?"[11] Have you ever had someone give you a reality check like Dorothy Parker?

It stings when someone gives you a reality check about how you might be too proud. Muhammad Ali was in his prime, and as he was

3

about to take off on an airplane flight, the flight attendant reminded him to fasten his seat belt. He said brashly, "Superman don't need no seat belt." The flight attendant quickly came back, "Superman don't need no airplane, either." Ali fastened his belt.[12] No one could doubt that the flight attendant handled that situation well.

It can also sting and hurt your pride when others make you feel slighted. We do not always consider others as equals. Consider Romans 12:16: "Consider everyone as equal, and don't think that you're better than anyone else. Instead associate with people who have no status. Don't think that you're so smart" (CEB). Imagine that there are two team captains choosing who will be on their team either at school or in the neighborhood. It makes you feel great if you are one of the first ones picked. It could also hurt your pride if you were one of the last ones picked. There were times in my childhood when being picked last did not make me feel that the captain who made the choice had much confidence in me.

THE WAY THE PHARISEE SAW GOD

It Seems the Pharisee Saw God as Being Indebted to Him

In his prayer, he told God how good he was. He thanked God that he was so good. Yes, he was good in the practice of the religious and legalistic ideals he upheld. But he was poor at looking within his own heart. His self-examination was lame because he never thought beyond himself. He appeared to be thanking God, but he was really praising himself. Yes, he mentioned God in his prayer, but God was not the object of his praise.

The Pharisee Prayed in a Way He Thought Would Be Pleasing to God

Fred B. Craddock notes that "While his prayer was in the spirit of Psalm 51, his life was offensive." Furthermore, "His prayer of thanksgiving is a modification of a common rabbinic prayer ('I thank thee that I am not…') joined to the spirit and content of Psalm 17:3-5)."[13] There is no question that though he may have been practicing what was the norm for Pharisees as to a prayer pattern, he came across as being arrogant.

In his book, *The 7 Deadly Sins*, Billy Graham notes that Lucifer's self-centeredness as described in Isaiah 14:12-15 was based upon PRIDE, which became his downfall.[14] The Pharisee is similar because he too exalted himself too highly. God created us to have pride within certain bounds. When our pride exceeds the bounds that God intended for it, we have the potential to become arrogant, presumptuous, and condescending.

There is a reciprocity factor to consider. George Buttrick made the point that, "What we think of ourselves and our neighbors stems from what we think about God."[15] All we have to do is look at the Pharisee in this parable to see how this rings true. Paul states that we are not to think of ourselves more highly of than we should (see Rom. 12:3). In the words of Jesus, the way we treat others is also a reflection of the way we treat God (see Matt. 25:40, 45).

There is the story about Dwight Moody, a nineteenth-century evangelist, who got put out with drunken passengers who sat across from him on a train. When they realized who he was, it seems that the two men tried to annoy him by singing hymns loudly. One of the train employees came by to punch the tickets of the passengers. Rev. Moody was disgusted because all the seats were taken and he had to contend with the drunken, swollen-eyed singer and his drunken pal. The train conductor, however, brought the drunken fellows to the baggage cart, nursed their wounds, and gave them something to eat. The next morning Rev. Moody became convicted of his behavior of the night before. He had begun to act like the Pharisee in the parable of the Pharisee and the publican. We too act like that without realizing that we have exalted ourselves while subordinating another or others.[16] Like Moody, it can be humbling to find out the ways in which we have acted like a Pharisee.

Gossip neglects the reciprocity factor. Gossip is one of the ways someone tries to exalt one's self at the expense of others. Why? The answer is that if people are talking about others, then they will be too busy to focus on their own faults. Everybody has faults. None of us has the right to exalt ourselves while subordinating or humiliating another or others—whether the method is by gossip or any other means. Gossiping has the character of selfish ambition because of its condescending agenda. The Bible tells us that we are to think of others by looking to their interests and not only to our own interests (see Phil. 2:4 NIV). Jesus Christ Himself exemplified this model (see Phil. 2:5-11).

THE WAY THE PHARISEE SAW OTHERS

He Saw the Publican Based upon His Reputation and Not His Character

The Pharisees categorized evildoers, adulterers, robbers, and tax collectors by the same rule (see Luke 18:11). This rule was that they were all sinners who were to be avoided. Many scholars have said that the point in this parable is that it is not the proud, but the humble and repentant, that God justifies with the gift of His grace. God's grace is something that no one can earn. All have sinned and have fallen short of the glory of God (see Rom. 3:23). The difference between the publican and the Pharisee is obvious. Jesus makes the point that it is often the people whom we consider to be beyond hope and help who are sometimes the most remorseful, while the proud are too self-righteous to see their need.

The Pharisees Thought That Their Understanding and Conduct Were Right

They were forever disagreeing with Jesus about His point of view and what God expected. If any of them were ever proven to be wrong, they were often too proud to admit their error and amend their ways. As mentioned earlier, Lucifer, whom we also call Satan, had the same problem with his pride.

How we view others says something about the way we view God. An anonymous person once said, "We use religion like a trolley car—we ride on it only when it is going our way." Were the Pharisees using their religion as a "trolley car"? Jesus welcomed those the Pharisees excluded, and that is why they were at odds with Jesus. It is interesting to note that Paul, who was a former Pharisee, became a follower of Jesus Christ. He gave fellow Christians this advice: "Consider everyone as equal, and don't think that you're better than anyone else. Instead associate with people who have no status. Don't think that you're so smart" (Rom. 12:16 CEB). The Pharisees often condemned sinners. However, those they condemned were often much more responsive to the gospel than the Pharisees. Do we treat others as equals?

When Jesus called the tax collector Levi, also known as Matthew, to come and be a disciple, Matthew got up and followed Jesus (see Mark 2:14). According to the theological perception of the Pharisees, tax collectors were considered to be just as worthy of reproach as all other sinners. It is important to note that tax collectors and publicans are one in the same. But listen to what happened after Matthew decided to follow Jesus.

> While Jesus was having dinner at Levi's house, many tax collectors and "sinners" were eating with him and his disciples, for there were many who followed him. When the teachers of the law who were Pharisees saw him eating with the "sinners" and tax collectors, they asked his disciples: "Why does he eat with tax collectors and 'sinners'?" On hearing this Jesus said to them, "It is not the healthy who need a doctor, but the sick. I have not come to call the righteous, but sinners.
> —Mark 2:15-17

With whom do we identify most in this parable: the Pharisee or the publican?

QUESTIONS:

1. How are we like the Pharisee?

   _____

   _____

   _____

   _____

2. How do we wrestle with pride?

   _____

   _____

   _____

   _____

3. What does the Bible say about pride?

   _____

   _____

   _____

   _____

4. Why do you think pride is necessary?

   _____

   _____

   _____

   _____

5. When does pride become excessive?

_____

_____

_____

_____

6. How do we see ourselves when we look in the mirror?

_____

_____

_____

_____

7. Do we do things that make others feel slighted?

_____

_____

_____

_____

8. How well do we treat others as equals?

_____

_____

_____

_____

9. Do we exercise any double standards? If so, why?

_____

_____

_____

_____

CHAPTER 2

THE SIN OF ENVY

Matthew 20:1-16

My first-grader came home and proudly reported to her dad that she was now officially a "Brownie." Not to be outdone, her three-year-old brother, Christopher, rushed up to Dad and proudly announced he was a cupcake!

—Kayleen J. Reusser, Bluffton, Indiana.[1]

Someone said Hollywood is not only a place where you must succeed but also a place where your friends must fail.

—Robert C. Shannon[2]

Envy is the sincerest form of flattery.
As rust corrupts iron, so envy corrupts man.[3]

Jealousy is nourished by doubt.

—French Proverb[4]

To jealousy, nothing is more frightful than laughter.[5]

A jealous man always finds more than he is looking for, envy shoots at others and wounds herself.[6]

—Madeleine de Scudery

If you want to travel light, take off all jealousies, selfishness, and fears.[7]

In a consumer society, there are inevitably two kinds of slaves: the prisoners of addictions and the prisoners of envy.

—Ivan Illich[8]

There is a Greek story about a man who killed himself through envy. His fellow citizens had erected a statue to one of their number who was a celebrated champion in the public games. But this man, a rival of the honored athlete, was so envious that he vowed that he would destroy that statue. Every night he went out into the darkness and chiseled at its base in an effort to undermine its foundation and make it fall. At last he succeeded. It did fall—but it fell on him. He fell, a victim to his own envy.[9]

ENVY CAN HIJACK our joy, our fellowship with others, and also our fellowship with God because it isolates us.[10] Envy is a bad thing to harbor in one's heart because it enables one to justify his or her resentment toward another or others. Envy therefore both isolates and insulates those who harbor it in their hearts.

In his book, *Fatal Attractions: Sermons on the Seven Deadly Sins,* William R. White notes that envy is competitive in that it is the part of us that is always comparing our outcome to that of others around us.[11] Sibling rivalries (often based on this type of conduct) are about envy. Genesis 4 serves as a good example of a sibling rivalry gone wrong because it was not only competitive, it was also deadly.

Genesis 4 contains the story of a rivalry between Cain and Abel. Cain was jealous of Abel's success. Abel gave the first fruits of his harvest, whereas Cain's offering slighted God's command. For that reason, when

Cain saw that Abel's offering was accepted and God rejected his, he killed his brother Abel. Notice, the first recorded murder occurs within the first book of the Bible, and the motive behind it was envy.

Envy has the potential to seize its victims while making them obsessed with "competing and comparing"[12] themselves and their outcomes to that of others around them. Consider the "competing and comparing" between other biblical siblings—Jacob and Esau (Gen. 27), Joseph and his brothers (Gen. 37), and the prodigal son and his elder brother (Luke 15:28-30). The parable of the workers in the vineyard (see Matt. 20:1-16) also addresses the issue of envy. Envy was at the root of the troublesome relationships between family members (siblings) as well as fellow employees.

Envy usually exists in three categories: talent, recognition, and possessions.

ENVY OF THE TALENTS OF OTHERS

There are people who are born with abilities that others may lack. When I went to college, I knew many guitar players who could play what they heard on the radio. I wished I had that talent. I went to high school with one of them. He did not play the guitar in high school. However, I saw him months later at college and he was playing an electric guitar. He sounded as if he had been playing all his life, when he had only been playing a few months. I honestly have to say that I admired his talent. Someone who can pick up on a talent like that is what we call "a natural."

There are others who may have potential talent that developed with lots of practice. Sometimes, there is a possibility for others to be jealous of those who appear to be naturals. It is harmless to wish you had the talent of another. It is quite another thing altogether to harbor resentment in one's heart that leads to spite. Feelings such as these, left unchecked, can be dangerous and sometimes turn deadly. Genesis 4 portrays how one brother's envy turned out to be deadly. Cain's resentment turned into spite. Cain was jealous of Abel because God accepted Abel's offering, whereas Cain's offering was inadequate. The Lord warned Cain that sin was waiting at the door for him, ready to strike him and master him (see Genesis 4:7). Unchecked, envy can become a consuming obsession as it did for Cain. Why is that? The answer is that unchecked envy is as dangerous as a house fire that is left to burn.

Halford Luccock once expounded upon the King James wording of Mark 7:22 where it mentions the "evil eye." He said that at first glance that phrase looks like superstition. The phrase "evil eye" means "...a jealous, grudging disposition."[13] Consider Proverbs 27:4, "Wrath is cruel, and anger is outrageous; but who is able to stand before envy?" (KJV). Luccock notes further that, "It can be a cardinal sin, for it has the power to sour life, to keep one from ever attaining the spirit of love which redeems."[14] Envy produces a "competitive spirit"[15] whereas love does not keep score (see 1 Cor. 13:4-8). Therefore, envy works against love as its promise is to propel one ahead. However, its reward is to rob its victims. Victims may win the contest in feeding the ego, but its payoff is misery because it has a narcissistic complex.

Consider the Greek mythological character of Narcissus. Narcissus was a young man who was stuck on himself. The end of the story is that one day he bent over a pool of water to take a drink and fell in love with his own reflection. He burned with grief as he saw that the reflection of his own loveliness was beyond his grasp. His conceit caused his death because he had become so obsessed with his own self-importance that nothing else mattered.[16] How can someone be in a relationship that is genuinely healthy if he or she is self-absorbed?

ENVY OF STATUS OR RECOGNITION OF OTHERS

People are often recognized for outstanding qualities that come from their talents. We choose leaders based on outstanding qualities, gifts, or charisma. Sometimes, there might be two or more people who are in the running for an office, a service award, a performance, or any kind of status where one's character and hard work are recognized. Yet, when you have two or more gifted leaders or people who are not only jealous, but also competitive of each other, the situation can prove harmful to the unity of the group. Even though we might not get chosen as a leader, everybody wants to feel important.

In the late 1800s, there were just two deacons in a small Baptist church in Mayfield County, Kentucky. The two deacons hated each other and always opposed one another. On a particular Sunday, one deacon put up a small wooden peg in the back wall so the minister could hang his hat. When the other deacon discovered the peg, he was outraged that he had not been consulted. The church took sides and eventually split. The departing group formed a new church, called, "The Anti-Peg Baptist Church."[17]

Oftentimes, there is hard work that goes into a project that may go unrecognized or be underrated. I once read a story about a newly elected political official who was told by one of his senior politicians that there were two kinds of horses—work horses and show horses. Work horses get the job done without worrying about who gets the credit, whereas show horses appeal to the limelight and publicity only to decelerate in pace after their moment of glory is over.[18] The underlying idea here is that humility is the key because it is not concerned with who gets the credit so much as it is of getting the job done.

Sometimes people become envious of another when the other is more successful. As implied earlier, envy can be a potential poison when it is tainted with a grudge against another whose success is praised as the highest. Just as a grudge resulting from envy was a dangerous thing for Cain, it is also dangerous for us. A grudge of that nature becomes dangerous because it gives sin an opportunity to wait at the door of our life and strike us (see Gen. 4:7). Jealousy is among the works of the flesh (see Gal. 5:20), whereas self-control is one of the fruits of the Holy Spirit (see Gal. 5:23). It is very unlikely that we can master our jealousy without God's help!

A chilling Jewish folktale tells of two merchants who owned shops across the street from one another. Each judged the day successful not on the basis of total sales, but on whether he made more than the other. Upon the completion of a sale, each would look across the street and mock the other. God decided to put an end to this nasty rivalry and sent an angel to visit one of the merchants.

"You can have anything you want in the world," the angel said. "It can be riches, wisdom, a long life, or many children. Just know that whatever you ask, your competitor will get twice as much. Thus, if you ask for $20,000, he will get $40,000. What is your wish?"

The merchant thought for a while before he answered, "Make me blind in one eye." Envy is as senseless as that.[19] How many people do we know that have envy that strong?

The Envy of Objects and Possessions

Sometimes people are envious of others because they covet what others have. The tenth commandment warns against this very thing: "You shall not covet your neighbor's house. You shall not covet your neighbor's wife, or his manservant or maidservant, his ox or donkey, or anything that belongs to your neighbor" (Exodus 20:17 NIV). But why is it that we are not to covet the belongings of another? Elizabeth R. Achtemeier sheds insight on the answer to this question. She says, "To deprive a man of his property is thus to deprive him of his God-given inheritance.... in the New Testament, covetousness is considered a hindrance to true worship and faith in God."[20] It is therefore no wonder that coveting the possessions of another has become a stumbling block in one's relationship with God. Second Samuel 11 depicts how David coveted Uriah's wife and broke the seventh commandment in both thought and deed. He also broke the sixth commandment, "You shall not murder" (Ex. 20:13) as he arranged Uriah's death; and the seventh, "You shall not commit adultery" (Ex. 20:14) as he had an affair with another man's wife; and the eighth "You shall not steal" (Ex. 20:15) as he stole Bathsheba, Uriah's wife, for himself. In looking at this story, we can see that what Elizabeth Achtemeier said about covetousness is true.

Envy robs its beholder of joy and hinders him from fellowship with God and others. White notes that envy is blind because its victim/ beholder can only see what one does not have instead of the blessings, abilities, and assets one has.[21] Consider the jealous workers in the parable of the workers in the vineyard (see Matt. 20:10-12). They objected to the landowner paying the same amount to those who had not worked as long or as hard as some had. Those workers who objected were envious of the landowner's generosity (see Matt. 20:15). The landowner responded to one of the workers by telling him to take his pay and go (see Matt. 20:14). Therefore, by his own objection of the landowner's generosity, this worker was jeopardizing his opportunity for future wages. The landowner's generosity is a mirror image of God and how He shares with us the undeserved gift of His grace.

Billy Graham gives us the following advice concerning envy: *Recognize it* for what it is. *Confess* your sinful struggle with it and *renounce* it. Then, *open your [our] heart[s] to the regenerating grace of Christ.*[22] It is easier said than done. When envy is a problem for us, we have to be wholeheartedly sincere in our confession or else our confession is half-hearted.

Jesus said that where our treasures are, our hearts will be also (see Matt. 6:21). Understanding this advice is important. The condition of our hearts depends upon how we see things. The eyes of envy are evil and they look into the darkness. Godly eyes see clearly because they strive to see things through God's vision where there is light (see Matt. 6:22-23). Paul gives us good and appropriate advice in Philippians 4:8-9.

From now on, brothers and sisters, if anything is excellent and if anything is admirable, focus your thoughts on these things: all that is true, all that is holy, all that is just, all that is pure, all that is lovely, and all that is worthy of praise. Practice these things: whatever you learned, received, heard, or saw in us. The God of peace will be with you. (CEB)

Having the kind of outlook that Paul mentions here cannot happen apart from our relationship with God, who can transform and renew us.

QUESTIONS

1. Have you ever found yourself secretly harboring a moment of envy in your life about something that someone else got and you didn't get?

   _____

   _____

   _____

   _____

2. Have you ever been the object of someone else's envy?

   _____

   _____

   _____

   _____

3. How have you observed envy in media, culture, movies, and celebrities?

   _____

   _____

   _____

   _____

4. What is the best way to handle envy in ourselves?

_____

_____

_____

_____

5. Have you ever observed envy that was destructive to another? If so, what did it cost him or her?

_____

_____

_____

_____

6. Would you rather be known as a work horse or a show horse?

_____

_____

_____

_____

7. Are you content with your lot?

_____

_____

_____

_____

8. Do we envy someone's success that came easily, when compared to the time it took us to climb to that level?

_____

_____

_____

_____

9. Have you reconciled with anyone that you once envied? If not, why not?

_____

_____

_____

_____

CHAPTER 3

THE SIN OF ANGER

Matthew 5:21-22

"It's wise to remember that anger is just one letter short of danger."

—Sam Ewing[1]

He that is soon angry dealeth foolishly.

—Prov. 14:17 KJV[2]

Be ye angry, and sin not: let not the sun go down upon your wrath.

—Eph. 4:26 KJV[3]

Let every man be swift to hear, slow to speak, slow to wrath.

—James 1:19 KJV[4]

Anger is a momentary madness.

—Horace, Epistles, Book I, epistle ii[5]

Anger helps straighten out a problem like a fan helps straighten out a pile of papers.

—Susan Marcotte[6]

Be ye angry, and sin not; therefore all anger is not sinful, because some degree of it, and on some occasions, is inevitable. But it becomes sinful and contradicts the rule of Scripture when it is conceived upon slight and inadequate provocation, and when it continues long.

—William Paley[7]

Anger is often more hurtful than the injury that caused it.

—American Proverb[8]

Life appears to me to be too short to be spent in nursing animosity or registering wrongs.

—Charlotte Brontë[9]

The proud man hath no God; the envious man hath no neighbor; the angry man hath not himself.

—Bishop Hall[10]

MY FATHER (WHO is now a retired pastor) once preached a revival for a congregation I served back in 1996. One of the illustrations he used was about a church where some of the congregation would not participate in Holy Communion because of the grudges they held with one another. This practice might sound a little odd, but it is the right thing to do under the circumstances. After all, the Bible says that we are to examine ourselves before we partake of the Lord's Supper (see 1 Cor. 11:28). By judging ourselves properly, we do not have to be disciplined by God. Otherwise, God disciplines us so that we will not be condemned with the world (see 1 Cor. 11:31-32). The point is that when we partake of Holy Communion, we are to do so as a forgiven and reconciled people because Christ gave His life for all of us.

The Bible tells us that it is okay to be angry, but not to sin (see Eph. 4:26). It is one thing to suffer a moment of anger. It is another thing altogether to nurture that anger and feed it until it becomes a grudge. A grudge incurs wrath. Jesus said that it was important for us to make things right with others before we could be right with God:

Therefore, if you are offering your gift at the altar and there remember that your brother has something against you, leave your gift there in front of the altar. First go and be reconciled to your brother; then come and offer your gift. Settle matters quickly with your adversary who is taking you to court. Do it while you are still with him on the way, or he may hand you over to the judge, and the judge may hand you over to the officer, and you may be thrown in prison. I tell you the truth, you will not get out until you have paid the last penny.

—Matt. 5:23-26 NIV

The longer we wait to be reconciled, the more we give the devil a chance to drive us further apart, as we might nurse our anger against one another until it becomes a grudge. Therefore, we must take care of the matter before the sun goes down (see Eph. 4:26).

I counsel every couple who wants me to officiate at their wedding. In doing so, I always ask every couple, "How do you handle conflict? Do you brood or do you seek reconciliation as soon as possible?" My sense of urgency behind these questions is based upon the biblical advice that cautions us not to let the sun go down on our anger (see Eph. 4:26). Yes, it is okay to be angry, but we are in danger of being sinfully angry if our anger is bigger than the cause itself. We are also in danger of being sinfully angry when we are still angry even after the point of conflict has been amended (see Eph. 4:26).

Anger harms our health, alienates our spirit, and withdraws our fellowship.

ANGER HARMS OUR HEALTH

Anger Can Harm Those Who Entertain Its Passion

Anger can cause us to feel on edge inside. It can trigger our adrenaline glands to go into overdrive, maintaining a constant readiness for argument and fighting. When our adrenaline glands are operating like that, our blood pressure increases, our stomachs get upset, and our bodies feel the results. Stress like that can do harm to our bodies.

23

In his book, *Love Is a Decision*, Gary Smalley notes: "Several researchers believe that some types of cancer result from the mega-doses of stress which unhealthy anger carries with it."[11] Smalley even notes that anger can contribute to heart problems, bleeding ulcers, depression, anxiety attacks, and a lowered resistance to colds and flu. That should not surprise us.

I remember one time (in 1985) when I got an ugly letter from the financial institution about my student loans when I was a sophomore in college. I was supposed to be deferred because I was in school. Furthermore, the letter they sent me stated that I would soon be in repayment status. I got so infuriated that I began to feel nauseous. It spoiled my appetite. I called the institution and explained I was still in school. It helped to resolve the confusion. There was no question that my reaction was greater than the problem itself.

Anger Can Cause Psychological and Emotional Problems

There is the story of a young lady who was anemic. No one could determine the cause. When she came back for her next appointment, the doctor (Paul Tournier) took another blood sample and noticed a change in its results. It was normal. If he had not kept accurate records, he might have thought he made a mistake. He asked the girl if there had been any change in her life since the last visit. She noted that she had forgiven someone against whom she had held a nasty grudge. All at once she felt as if she could say yes to life again. Her physical problem of anemia went away when her attitude changed.[12] Our anger can do the same kind of thing to us when we nurse its negative energy and fuel its passion.

ANGER ALIENATES OUR SPIRIT

Anger Can Cloud One's Perception

Sometimes the word "anger" and the word "mad" are used interchangeably. Horace said that "Anger is short madness." It has been said that you can tell a lot about a man by the size of what makes him angry. Therefore, if a little and insignificant matter provokes someone and makes one mad, then that person is a lot less likely to be levelheaded.

There is the story about a man who got angry at a cat. To even the score, he set the cat's tail on fire. In the meantime, the cat ran through his barn in anguish. The cat continued to run from building to building, setting other buildings on fire.[13] There can be no doubt that his anger made him temporarily insane.

Despite its duration and alienation, there are two kinds of anger. There are two Greek words that describe anger well. William Barclay describes both. *Thumos* describes an instantaneous anger that comes and goes quickly. *Orge* describes the type of anger that lingers.[14] The latter is the type of anger with negative energy that we nurture (unnecessarily) over the course of time. It is the kind of anger that has the power to consume anyone who harbors it.

Many times I have heard statements about others said in moments of anger. How often have we said things in anger that we would not have said under normal circumstances? Consider the way Jesus describes anger in Matthew 5:21-22. That is where Jesus expounds upon the sixth commandment, "You shall not murder" (Ex. 20:13). In this scripture passage, Jesus describes how "the tongue has the power of life and death" (Prov. 18:21). Therefore, saying *raca* as described by the King James Version is equated with calling someone an "idiot" according to the Common English Bible. Saying something scornful and intentional like that is insulting and is not acceptable according to the Bible. In the time of Jesus' earthly ministry, people were literally held accountable by the Sanhedrin.[15]

John Wesley expounded on the Matthew 5:22 passage. He said, "Our Lord specified three degrees of murder, each liable to a sorer punishment than the other: not indeed from men, but from God."[16] As time passes, people might not recall the exact words of what someone said in anger, but they will most certainly remember how those stinging words, spoken in anger, made him or her feel. Just as we cannot put toothpaste back in the tube, we cannot take back our words once they are spoken.

To call someone a "fool" or "moron" (which is Greek for the word fool) is to put one's self in danger of hell's fires! As Barclay put it: "So, then, Jesus insists that the gravest thing of all is to destroy a man's reputation and to take his good name away. No punishment is too severe for the malicious tale bearer or the gossip over the teacups, which murders people's reputations. Such conduct, in the most literal sense, is a hell-deserving sin."[17] Sometimes we are hell-bent by the way we talk about each other, or to each other, in anger.

Whether we say something in a moment of anger (*thumos*) or are continually saying things out of anger over the course of time (*orge*), the point is that we need to watch what we say: "For by your words you will be acquitted, and by your words you will be condemned" (Matt. 12:37). Therefore, we should not make light of the words we speak. Our words can wound or kill someone's spirit. We can be murderers at heart by the very words we speak. As mentioned earlier, "the power of the tongue is life and death."

ANGER WITHDRAWS US FROM THE FELLOWSHIP OF GOD AND OTHERS

It separates us from the community. There is nothing wrong with being mad about the injustices we see in this world. There are things and behavior patterns in this world that are not acceptable in the eyes of God. We should not condone those things. What we have to guard against is nurturing anger that can consume, dominate, embitter, and even isolate us because of how it causes a "closed spirit."

To be mad about something that God would not approve of is what we call righteous indignation. Jesus had justified anger (righteous indignation) when he got mad at the moneychangers in the temple because they turned God's house into a den of thieves and robbers (see Matt. 21:13).

Anger creates in us a closed spirit. In his book, *Love Is a Decision*, Gary Smalley talks about how anger can cause a "closed spirit" between one and his/her spouse.[18] He notes that the kind of things that close a person's spirit are "belittling others, speaking harshly, being unwilling to admit when we are wrong, taking people for granted, sarcasm and insensitive jokes, being rude to someone in front of others, and slighting the importance of another's needs."[19] As mentioned earlier, anger harms our health, alienates our spirit, and withdraws our fellowship. Therefore, it is important that we handle our anger rather than letting it handle us. Unchecked anger can be divisive and destructive.

QUESTIONS

1. It has been said that *anger* is one letter short of *danger*. Why and how is anger dangerous?

   _____

   _____

   _____

   _____

2. Have you ever known someone who was defeated by the "danger" of their anger?

   _____

   _____

   _____

   _____

3. How do you manage anger?

   _____

   _____

_____

_____

4. How does anger effect relationships?

_____

_____

_____

_____

5. How can anger affect our health?

_____

_____

_____

_____

6. Do you know anyone who ever had to take anger management classes?

_____

_____

_____

_____

7. How is your temper now, compared to what it was like when you were a child?

_____

_____

_____

_____

8. Have you ever experienced road rage? Did it get you a ticket?

_____

_____

_____

_____

CHAPTER 4

THE SIN OF SLOTHFULNESS

Matthew 25:26-28, Revelation 3:15-16

Idleness is the Dead Sea that swallows all virtues. Be active in business, that temptation may miss her aim; the bird that sits is easily shot.

—Benjamin Franklin[1]

The outlook for our country lies in the quality of its idleness.

—Irwin Edman[2]

An idle man's brain is the devil's workshop.

—John Bunyan[3]

Untilled soil, however fertile it may be, will bear thistles and thorns; so it is with man's mind.

—Saint Teresa of Ávila[4]

Be always employed about some rational thing, that the devil find thee not idle.

—Saint Jerome[5]

By the streets of "By and By" one arrives at the house of "Never."
—Miguel de Cervantes[6]

With enough "ifs" we could put Paris into a bottle.
—French proverb[7]

Laziness grows on people; it begins in cobwebs and ends in iron chains.
—Thomas Fowell Buxton[8]

A lazy boy and a warm bed are difficult to part.
—Danish Proverb[9]

You cannot kill time without injuring eternity.
—Anonymous [10]

God gives every bird its food, but He does not throw it into the nest.
—Josiah G. Holland [11]

I ONCE HEARD a story about a Catholic priest who felt God putting a sense of urgency upon him to go and see a parishioner. He delayed, then finally he headed out the door. Then he changed his mind and came back. He had lunch with his parishioner the day before. Since everything seemed okay, he second guessed himself about his sense of urgency to go check on his parishioner. It was later discovered that his parishioner committed suicide. Could he have stopped this tragedy if he had followed his gut feeling? Maybe he could have and maybe not. He felt guilty about his procrastination. The priest never got over his feelings of guilt. Procrastination is similar to slothfulness because both neglect duty.

It is possible for someone to be physically busy while spiritually apathetic. Billy Graham, in his book *The 7 Deadly Sins,* makes the point that, "Spiritual laziness is not only a sin against God—it is a sin against yourself. It measures the distance between what you ought to be and what you actually are. It shows the difference between the person you are and the person you could be."[12] That raises an interesting point about the two kinds of sin that keep us from reaching our God-given potential. There are the sins of commission, where we do things that we should have avoided doing. There are also the sins of omission, where we leave undone the things we should not avoid.

We normally think of slothfulness in terms of physical inactivity and irresponsibility. It is possible to be slothful in our spiritual lives as well. Slothfulness involves the sins of omission that have at least three levels. First, there is the individual level; second, the domestic and group level; and finally, the congregational and church level.

THE INDIVIDUAL LEVEL

Slothfulness Involves Health Matters

If we are neglectful of our health, it could prove to be costly in the long run. There is the story about a man who loved carrot juice. He drank it all the time. However, upon the results of a medical examination, he was warned not to drink it any more due to the fact that it would harm his already damaged liver. He continued to neglect the warning, and it eventually cost him his life.

Slothfulness Involves Duty

There is the story of a mechanic who failed to tighten the screw on the oil pan of a car. The new car developed an oil leak following that oil change. The owner became suspicious. He took the car back and questioned the mechanic about what was wrong. In embarrassment, the head honcho of the dealership discovered that the car developed a leak because the assigned mechanic failed to tighten a screw on the oil pan tightly enough. Such a simple mistake might have cost both the owner and the mechanic unnecessary trouble and expense if the engine had been damaged.

Slothfulness Is Spiritual

People often make excuses as to why they do not attend church. Church attendance is not the only concern. There are people who neglect their prayer and devotional life. The Bible tells us that where our hearts are, our treasure will be also (see Matt. 6:21). The Bible also tells us that God knows what it is that we are in need of even before we ask Him (see Matt. 6:8), but oftentimes we find ourselves lacking because we have not asked God (see James 4:2).

Slothfulness Can Be Habit Forming

I have often heard people say that Sunday is the only day they have for themselves, which is why they stay at home in bed, go golfing, fishing, or hunting. Although those might seem like one-time excuses, they derive from a lack of attention that we should give to God, and that can cause bad habits.

Slothfulness Is Moral

In his book, *Fatal Attractions: Sermons on the Seven Deadly Sins,* William R. White notes the sin of slothfulness in the life of Albert Speer.

> In his autobiography *Inside the Third Reich,* Albert Speer confesses that he was so obsessed with his position as Hitler's chief architect that he became blind to the slaughter of the Jews. Speer was, by all accounts, a brilliant man who did such a spectacular job of organizing Germany's industry that his efforts alone may have prolonged the war by two years.
>
> Born of a prosperous and professional family, Albert Speer was a fine husband and a wonderful parent. He was a liberal who certainly did not hate Jewish people. He saw his position in the Third Reich as a great professional opportunity. Though thousands were murdered or imprisoned before his eyes, Speer claims he was oblivious to the

horrors going on around him. He was just an architect doing his job. The name for this deadly vice is sloth. People often confuse sloth with idleness.[13]

THE DOMESTIC LEVEL

We Could Use the Term "Domestic" to Mean Those in Our Own Family

When we consider the parable of the lost coin in Luke 15:8-10, we can relate that story to carelessness for something that was in our care. We can even relate to how we might have been careless with others. There are people who live in the same house, and some are lost partially due to the carelessness of others.

There are married couples living in potential conflict because they neglect their relationship with a spouse. Healthy relationships need to be nurtured. As Warren Wiersbe once wisely said, "Marriage creates the union, but it takes daily love and devotion to maintain the communion."[14] Healthy relationships do not happen by default. It is important for married couples to work on their relationship. When I counsel couples for marriage, I suggest that every couple have a "date night" once a week if possible, even after they are married.

Suppose one's spouse forgets a very important date, like a birthday or anniversary. You can bet he/she will have a tough time living it down. The fact that something important was overlooked can send a message that the one who forgot did not consider it important enough to remember.

There are families where the children can get lost in spirit because of their unmet needs. Children need to be nurtured. As children become teens, parents usually strive to relate to them in a way that is fruitful. I once had a church member who took up go-cart racing with his son during his teenage years. Through go-cart racing, that father established a strong bond with his son, who went on to become a highway patrolman.

The father knew the bond that he developed with his son would not have happened by default.

The Term "Domestic" Can Also Refer to Our Own Country

Many times we hear about how we can help those in third-world countries. At the same time, it is sometimes possible for us have tunnel vision concerning the needs of those in our own communities. When we slight their needs, it seems to send a message that we do not care.

THE CHURCH AND CONGREGATIONAL LEVEL

We have a harvest that is plentiful, yet we are still in need of workers (see Matt. 9:37). The church is in the world, and she needs to witness to the world about God's love, grace, and mercy. However, sometimes we as the church fail when we are judgmental and merciless or indifferent. Sometimes, we act more like the world and less like Christ. In the words of Max Lucado, "We might be near the cross, but far away from Christ."[15] At times, we might resemble the soldiers who gambled for Christ's clothing at the foot of the cross (see John 19:23-24). How will others know that we are Christ's disciples keeping the commandment to love one another if we are apathetic rather than loving?

Matthew 25 has three parables about three different angles of apathy that are warnings to the church about its responsibility. Matthew 25:1-13 is the parable of the ten virgins. It is about people who were ready as well as those who procrastinated until it was too late to do something about salvation. Matthew 25:14-30 gives the parable of the talents. It is a story about how we are to use the gifts God gave us by applying them without withholding any potential. Matthew 25:31-46 is the story of the sheep and the goats, and it is a story about hospitality. It illustrates that the way we treat the least of these—strangers, the hungry, the thirsty, those in need of clothes, the sick, and those in prison—is also the way we are treating our Lord.

There is a story about a Jew who reminded a Lithuanian woman of her Christian responsibility.

On September 27, 1941, 3,400 Jews in the little Lithuanian town of Eisiskes were rounded up by special SS units and were driven to a Jewish cemetery. There they forced to strip and were then shot at the edge of previously dug trenches.

A 16-year old boy named Zvi Michalowski fell into the pit unharmed a split second before the bullets killed those standing with him, including his father. When night fell, he climbed out of the mass grave and ran naked, covered with blood, to a nearby house of a peasant. In response to the boy's anguished plea for asylum, the peasant shouted, "Jew, go back to the grave where you belong!" and slammed the door in his face. There was the same response at several other doors.

Finally, Michalowski came to the home of an old widow he knew. She, too, drove him off, waving a firebrand at him as if exorcising an apparition. In utter despair, Michalowski returned to the widow saying to her, "I am your Lord Jesus Christ. I came down from the cross. Look at me—the blood, the pain, the suffering of the innocent." Crossing herself, the old woman fell at his bloody feet, then let him in, washed and fed him for the three days that he asked to remain. The young man subsequently was able to join a group of partisans in the forest and survived the war. Perhaps the woman suddenly remembered that, "Inasmuch as you did it unto the least of these my brethren, you did it unto me" and sheltered the Lord who came in the guise of a needy Jewish boy! You will encounter Jesus as you reach out to those around you. Like the woman, you will discover that Jesus is served when any hungry, hurting, or homeless person is served.[16]

Many things are made obvious by this story. First, this woman knew Christ. Second, in rejecting the young man, she was rejecting Jesus, until she was convicted of her own apathy to the point of compassion.

Third, she had the means, the "talent" with which to help him. Though she rejected him at first, she repented and did the right thing when she fed and sheltered him. Before we condemn this woman, we need to remember that sometimes the church fails to minister to others in need. This is the sin of slothfulness. That is the same sin the church in Laodicea was admonished for because it was neither cold nor hot, but "lukewarm" (see Rev. 3:15-16). To be "lukewarm" is to be indecisive and indifferent and compromising as opposed to being committed and passionate to our responsibility as Christ's disciples.

QUESTIONS

1. How do we wrestle with the sin of slothfulness in our own lives? Has our slothfulness ever inconvenienced someone else or let them down?

_____

_____

_____

_____

2. How do we see others wrestle with slothfulness?

_____

_____

_____

_____

3. Have you ever known anyone whose life was affected by this sin?

_____

_____

_____

_____

4. How do you feel when you encounter someone who is obviously lazy in customer service?

_____

_____

_____

_____

5. How well do you handle slowpoke drivers? Do you react with horn blowing?

_____

_____

_____

_____

6. When you were in school, did you ever procrastinate and turn in an assignment late without penalty?

_____

_____

_____

_____

7. Have you ever made it a goal not to procrastinate?

_____

_____

_____

_____

8. What will happen if a congregation is slothful in its mission to make disciples?

_____

_____

_____

_____

9. How is idleness dangerous to us in our spiritual life?

_____

_____

_____

_____

CHAPTER 5

THE SIN OF GREED

Matthew 6:24, I Timothy 6:10

Augustine (A.D. 354-430) said, "God wants to give us something, but cannot, because our hands are full—there's nowhere for him to put it." When we feel as though God's blessings are missing from our lives, we need to examine our hands and see if they are open to receive, or clutched around something that we refuse to let go.[1]

Earthly goods are given to be used, not to be collected .... Hoarding is idolatry.[2]

One day, in Springfield, a neighbor of Lincoln's was drawn to his door by the sound of crying children. He saw Lincoln passing by with his two sons both crying lustily. "What is the matter with the boys?" asked the man. "The same that is the matter with the whole world!" answered Lincoln. "I have three walnuts, and each boy wants two."[3]

The sun is 865,000 miles across, but the smallest coin can block out the sun if you hold it close enough to your eye![4]

The great Roman Marcus Aurelius said, "The true worth of a man is to be measured by the objects he pursues."[5]

It has been said that just as a circle can never fill a triangle so the heart of greed is never satisfied. Its hunger is never filled; its thirst is never quenched. No wonder we are so often warned against it.[6]

The earth provides enough for every man's need but not for every man's greed.[7]

YEARS AGO, I attended a luncheon that was hosted and paid for by a law firm. As they fed us, they also told us about legal matters pertaining to family issues. Among the topics they discussed was the subject of divorce. Now, keep in mind that this is a Christian law firm we are talking about. They declared that they were Christian both by profession and practice. They saw their practice of law as a ministry. Rather than escalating the arguments involved with a divorce, they declared that they try to help couples who are contemplating a divorce to seek reconciliation. They were also helpful to those couples who did pursue a divorce. In short, they declared that they avoided the path of greed that other lawyers allegedly embraced by trying to make as much money as they could from the spouse of their client. Just because someone is a lawyer it does not automatically mean that he or she is greedy. It must be said that greed has more to do with a person's character than how that person makes a living.

Greed in general is about getting what you want monetarily or materially unethically at the expense of others. Greed is about money, but it is also about even more than money. Greed is about having what is adequate and still not being satisfied. If the Lord is our Shepherd, then we shall not be in want (see Ps. 23:1). The world has the philosophy that, "He who dies with the most toys wins." As a former sales clerk, I used to sell t-shirts that had that statement printed on them. The Bible tells us a different view. "Then Jesus said to his disciples, 'If anyone would come after me, he must deny himself and take up his cross and follow me. For whoever wants to save his life will lose it, but whoever loses his life for me will find it. What good will it be for a man if he gains the whole world, yet forfeits his soul? Or what can a man give in exchange for his soul?'" (Matt. 16:24-26 NIV).

Greed will make one self-serving rather than humble. The Bible also tells us that we must think of others as better than ourselves in order to keep our humility in perspective so that we will be able to avoid selfish ambition (see Phil. 2:3).

Greed is idolatrous, obsessive, and excessive. In the end, it always cheats its subjects who think that they will cheat the system.

GREED IS IDOLATROUS

An idol usurps God's place and authority. My Old Testament professor from seminary, Dr. Efird, also taught New Testament. In his book *The New Testament Writings*, he said, "Idols in reality are only extensions of the self. Therefore, when one is an idolater, that person is simply worshipping oneself.[8] Idolatry always serves to get its subjects into trouble. Anything that takes the place of the reverence God should have in our lives becomes an idol.

Idolatry seeks pleasure. When we make something an idol, it breaks both the first and second commandments. The first commandment says: "You shall have no other gods before me" (Ex. 20:3). The second commandment says: "You shall not make for yourself an idol in the form of anything in heaven above or earth beneath or in the waters below. You shall not bow down to them and worship them; for I, the Lord your God, am a jealous God, punishing the children for the sin of the fathers to the third and fourth generation of those who hate me, but showing love to a thousand generations of those who love me and keep my commandments" (Exodus 20:4 NIV).

Why then do we break these commandments? The answer is because we sometimes put other things in the place of God. The love of money is perhaps the biggest potential flaw (see 1 Tim. 6:10). The lack of being content with "our lot in life" is but another flaw (see Phil. 4:11-13). Yet, we worry about money and materialism. Jesus told us how to keep things in perspective when He said, "But seek first his kingdom and his righteousness, and all these things will be given to you as well. Therefore do not worry about tomorrow, for tomorrow will worry about itself. Each day has enough trouble of its own" (Matt. 6:33-34 NIV).

GREED IS OBSESSIVE

In the context of greed, the word "obsession" seems to indicate an unruly and incorrigible desire. That is the way greed is. It is a desire that is beyond one's capacity to reckon with through reason when it has become an obsession. Billy Graham quoted Charles Kingsley, who once said, "If you wish to be miserable think about yourself: about what you want, what you like, what respect people ought to pay you—and then to you nothing will be pure. You will spoil everything you touch. You will make misery for yourself out of everything good. You will be as wretched as you choose."[9] Who wants that kind of King Midas touch? How many of us are suffering from the consequences of greedy leaders who should have known better?

There are some people who believe they can get something for nothing. They believe that they can cheat the system without having to steal to do it. Gambling is their vice. I watched a guy waste ten dollars at a bowling alley on a video poker machine. He was infuriated when he spent his last quarter. For people of that character, poverty can become their fate because of their greed.

Gambling hurts more than the gambler. As I mentioned earlier, greed is about getting what you want monetarily and materially at the unethical expense of others. The ones who squander their paychecks on gambling sometimes do so at the expense of others. I knew a woman who divorced her husband because of his gambling habit that caused great hardships on him and his family. He had become a slave of greed.

Gambling is obsessive in that it can exploit the people who become enslaved to it. Those who own the video poker machines and online gambling sites contribute to this problem. Gambling is not a living organism that exploits others, and any form of gambling can become exploitive. No, gambling is a sickness—a hunger for more than we need. It exists in the lives of those who cater to its poison.

Yes, there are some who might buy lottery tickets every now and then with the same type of attitude that we buy a raffle ticket. However, when one becomes obsessed with beating the system in taking a chance, then it becomes possible for one to get hooked on gambling. A gambler always thinks, "Just one more time, and I'll win." The problem for a gambler is that it becomes one more time and one more time and one more time and so on until he or she is out of money.

GREED IS EXCESSIVE

Greed never looks beyond itself. In Luke 12:13-21 Jesus tells the parable about the rich fool. He was happy with his harvest. He had more than enough. In fact, he had a harvest so big that he could not store all of it in the existing barns that he had. He decided he would tear down his old barns and build bigger buildings. He did not think about the needy that he might help because he was too selfish and greedy. He was too busy storing up treasures on earth rather than in heaven. "Treasure in heaven" refers to sharing the abundance of our God-given blessing with others who are less fortunate than we are (according to Mark 10:21).

When Hurricane Hugo hit the coast of South Carolina some supplies were scarce. I was in my first semester of seminary when the hurricane struck. I remember coming home that weekend to see the damage it had done. Profiteering proved to be an ironic twist. You would think that the crisis would have made people more sympathetic. Actually, it caused some local businesses to show their true "greedy" colors. Like the rich fool in Luke 12:13-21, there were businesses that were selfish. Like the rich fool, the profiteers could not avoid judgment. By the standards of

45

the kingdom of God, the rich fool was in trouble because he was poor as far as "treasures in heaven" were concerned. To add insult to injury, that very night God would demand his life. The profiteers faced the judgment of dissatisfied customers, who took their business elsewhere.

God calls us to look beyond ourselves. Charles Dickens once wrote a wonderful Christmas story entitled *A Christmas Carol.* It is probably common knowledge that Ebenezer Scrooge, who was sorely scornful toward his fellow man, was the main character of the story. He was much like the "rich fool" in the parable Jesus told (Luke 12:13-21). However, Scrooge's story has a happy ending in that while he was selfish, stingy, and greedy, he was made to look beyond himself.

The change in his life was brought about by the visitation of three ghosts: the ghost of Christmas past, the ghost of Christmas present, and the ghost of Christmas future. The third ghost got his attention when Scrooge was made to look at his own future—a grave with his name on it. The point of the story was that he would die without having left the world a better place. Nobody wants to have a life that does not matter.

Ernest A. Fitzgerald in his book, *Keeping Pace: Inspirations in the Air,* observes that people respond one of three ways when someone dies: "The first way is negative in that people do not grieve much when their unruly and incorrigible enemies die. Two thousand years ago, King Herod was such a person. He decreed that 300 prominent citizens be executed when he died because he knew that not many, if any, would grieve his death."[10]

The second way is a little better. The people of this category are nice but complacent. They are neutral. They are neither cold nor hot like the people of Laodicea (see Rev. 3:15-16). As Fitzgerald says, "Such people are usually well-liked, but seldom respected. They are popular, but not trustworthy."[11] He continues to say that these are people who "look out for their own best interests." Therefore, when they die, they are not missed because of their lack of contributions and because they remained "neutral."

46

Finally, there is the last group with a third way people respond to others' passing. Someone once asked Lincoln how he would like to be remembered. He did not dwell on his success as a politician. In fact, he never even mentioned his presidency as he answered the question. He simply said that he wanted to be remembered as someone who, "plucked a thistle and planted a flower where a flower would grow."[12] Ebenezer Scrooge went from the second to the third category because finally he got to where he looked beyond himself. He became a sympathetic and a compassionate person.

Jesus said that foxes had holes and that birds of the air had nests, but He, "the Son of Man had no place to lay His head" (Matt. 8:20). In fact, Jesus did not even own a place in which to be buried. It was Joseph of Arimathea who buried Jesus in a rich man's tomb (see John 19:38-40). Jesus gave us His all. For our sakes He became poor so that through His poverty we might become rich (see 2 Cor. 8:9). In living life that way, during the time of His earthly ministry, He set the example of a humble way of life. His life and witness on earth make the point that we can make a difference in this world without materialism. He truly showed us what it means to "store up treasures in heaven."

Greed seeks a crown without a cross. Its price is greater than its reward. Those who seek to cheat the system by thinking they can get ahead will, in the end, get cheated by the god of greed they worship.

Consider "The Pardoner's Tale" from Geoffrey Chaucer's *The Canterbury Tales* (–14th Century). In that story we are told about three young men who leave a tavern and discover that Death has killed a man. They swear to each other that they will slay Death if they catch him. While walking up the road, they are warned by an elderly man that this traitor Death is by the oak tree ahead. At the tree they find eight bushels of gold. Two of the three travelers are brothers. They draw straws to see who should return to town to get bread and wine. While one is gone on the errand, the two brothers plot to stab him to death and divide the gold between themselves. Little did they know that he

THE SEVEN DEADLY SINS

had two specially prepared poison drinks to serve them upon his return so that he could keep the gold for himself. As he returns, they stab him. Then they drink their drinks and they, themselves, die from the poison. All three thought they could cheat death. They catered to greed, and in the end it killed all of them. With a story such as this, it is no wonder that greed was, and is, considered to be a deadly sin.[13]

There is no such thing as a crown without a cross for those who are Christian. Again, the world declares that, "He who dies with the most toys wins." But Jesus says in the Bible, "For whoever wants to save his life will lose it, but whoever loses his life for me and for the gospel will save it. What good is it for a man to gain the whole world, yet forfeit his soul? Or what can a man give in exchange for his soul?" (Mark 8:35-37). It is not money, but the love of money, that is evil (see 1 Tim. 6:10). If we choose to live the way Jesus showed us, we will choose life. Choosing Christ means we must deny ourselves, take up our cross, and follow in His footsteps (see Mark 8:34).

QUESTIONS

1. How do you see greed active in the world today?

   _____

   _____

   _____

   _____

2. Have you ever known a well-known celebrity who was conquered by greed?

   _____

   _____

_____

_____

3. How have you wrestled with greed in your own life?

_____

_____

_____

_____

4. How do you feel about greedy leaders who should know better?

_____

_____

_____

_____

5. Can greedy people reform and be transformed?

_____

_____

_____

_____

6. Do we wrestle with forgiving greedy people who have cost us because of their mistakes?

_____

_____

_____

_____

7. Do we view lawyers and other greedy people in power the same way the Pharisees perceived the tax collectors?

_____

_____

_____

_____

8. How has greed impacted the church historically?

_____

_____

_____

_____

9. Have you ever encountered the injustice of a business going up on prices during a crisis?

_____

_____

_____

_____

CHAPTER 6

THE SIN OF GLUTTONY

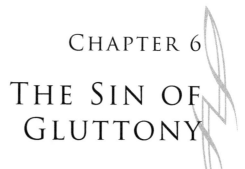

1 Corinthians 11:17-22

It is written, "One does not live by bread alone, but by every word that comes from the mouth of God."

—Matthew 4:4 NRSV[1]

His eye is bigger than his belly. The mouth has a little hole, but it can swallow house and roof.

—Yiddish Proverb[2]

At the end of every diet, the path curves back toward the trough.

—Mason Cooley[3]

Diets are for those who are thick and tired of it.

—Mary Tyler Moore[4]

The waist is a terrible thing to mind.

—Tom Wilson, "Ziggy"[5]

One should eat to live, not live to eat.

—Molière[6]

The appetite grows by eating.

—François Rabelais[7]

A hungry man is not a free man.

—Adlai Stevenson[8]

Satan, like a good fisherman, baits his hook according to the appetite of the fish.[9]

It is my conviction that a very large part of mankind's ills and of the world's misery is due to the rampant practice of trying to feed the soul with the body's food.

—Frank Farrell[10]

Whether therefore ye eat, or drink, or whatsoever ye do, do all to the glory of God.

—1 Cor. 10:31 KJV[11]

The way to a man's heart is through his stomach.

Better is a dinner of herbs where love is, than a stalled ox and hatred therewith.

—Prov. 15:17 KJV[12]

GLUTTONY IS THE sin of over-indulgence. It is the sin of eating too much. It is also about selfishness. In his book, *Fatal Attractions: Sermons on the Seven Deadly Sins*, William R. White said that, "Gluttony connects us neither with others or with God. It is a solitary act that defeats rather than enhances community."[13] First Corinthians 11:17-22 deals with a community in which the Lord's Supper was served. The sin of gluttony was evident. Some went ahead with their supper and others went hungry and still others became drunk (see 1 Cor. 11:21). The meal resembled the Lord's Supper, but it was insensitive to those who were excluded. The Lord's Supper is symbolic of reconciliation, unity, and forgiveness.

Years ago, there was an article in the Anderson *Independent Mail* newspaper about a man by the name of Charles Steinmetz. Two weeks before his death, he weighed 670 pounds. Two weeks later, when he died, he weighed 740 pounds. He gained 70 pounds in two weeks. Before he died, he complained about lung congestion. It took 16 men to load him into a delivery truck for the trip to the hospital. Steinmentz was 68 inches tall and 76 inches around. He said he just could not stop eating. He died at the age of 38 of lung congestion. Obviously, he was hungering for more than food.[14]

Gluttony is an excessive, solitary act that isolates and destroys fellowship.

GLUTTONY IS EXCESSIVE

Using food to compensate for unresolved restlessness is always a bad choice. The Bible tells us that man shall not live by bread alone, but by every word that proceeds out of the mouth of God (see Deut. 8:3). Richard Bach once wrote a book entitled *Jonathon Livingston Seagull.* The book depicted a seagull that stood out from the rest of the crowd because unlike his fellow seagulls that flew to eat, Jonathon ate to fly.[15] His character seems to be an illustrative symbol of the way man simply cannot live by bread alone.

GLUTTONY WILL NOT RESOLVE RESTLESSNESS

No amount of stress eating will ever resolve our restlessness. St. Augustine once said, "Our souls are restless until they find rest in God." Jesus tells us not to worry about our needs because God will take care of us just as God takes care of the birds of the air (see Matt. 6:25-34). We must realize that God is the source of all our needs. Psalm 23:1-2 puts it this way: "The Lord is my shepherd; I shall not want" (KJV). Gluttony cannot resolve restlessness because we cannot substitute food for the guidance that only the Good Shepherd, Jesus Christ, can give us.

Overeating can cause problems. Aside from indigestion, nausea, and vomiting that can result from overeating, there are other problems caused by overeating, including weight gain and heart and respiratory ailments. Just look at the story of Charles Steinmetz for proof. His chronic problem of overeating caused him to have not only weight problems, but also congested lungs.

We do not know if Charles Steinmetz had faith in God, because the story did not tell us. He said that he just could not stop eating. He became a slave to the food he ate. He lived to eat. For Steinmetz, eating was an addiction.

How often do our eyes get larger than our stomachs? Almost anyone who eats at an all-you-can-eat buffet has a tendency to overeat. The reason is that we want to get our money's worth. A friend once told me that our stomachs are at least seven minutes behind our brains in processing the sensation of being full. That explains why all of a sudden we don't start feeling full until one or more trips back to the buffet line. When I was five years old, I overate at a church dinner. I had made at least three trips to the food-serving tables. My stomach was definitely "behind my brain" that day. Needless to say, my father was not enthused when I tossed my cookies on the floorboard of the car on the way home.

Gluttony Is a Solitary Act

People sometimes substitute eating for the emptiness they are feeling. As mentioned earlier, Charles Steinmetz noted that he "just could not stop eating." There was something that compelled him to eat the way he did. Whatever was missing in his life made him a slave to gluttony. It appeared to be more than just physical hunger. It seemed to have been a spiritual hunger that he nurtured with physical food. It was something he tried to handle on his own.

54

Gluttony is a selfish act. It isolates one from concern for others in their midst. Now, before we point our fingers at the heavier people around us, let us remember that we ourselves are guilty of gluttony. How many times have we seen commercials or infomercials asking our help to support the feeding of the starving? How many times did our parents tell us to eat what was put in front of us because of the starving children around the world? How often did we think of those starving children when we were at an all-you-can eat buffet? How often do we find forgotten and spoiled leftovers in the fridge that we did not finish? I have to admit, I too am guilty of the charges mentioned above.

GLUTTONY DEFEATS FELLOWSHIP

We cannot have fellowship with food. God made us as creatures in need of Him and in need of each other. All of us hunger for community. I once stood in line with my parents at Jackson's Cafeteria on Sunday after church back in 1986. I happened to notice that the woman behind me was hiding her tears. I felt the Spirit move me to speak. I did not even plan my dialogue. I let God speak through me. First, I just spoke about the weather. I came to find out that the woman (in her late forties) was divorced and was about to walk out of the restaurant because she hated to eat alone. She explained to me how she felt (depressed) and why—eating alone. She then said she knew the Lord had put it on my heart to speak to her. She began to smile.

God created us to be companions to one another. Romans 12:5 says, "So in Christ we who are many form one body, and each member belongs to all the others (NIV)." Romans 12:5 helps us understand that God did not create us to stand alone. Although we might seek some time for solitude, we all need the fellowship of God and others. It is through our fellowship that we help others with their burdens and fulfill the law of Christ (see Gal. 6:2).

There are three Greek nouns for fellowship. One of them is *Koinonia*. Koinonia denotes a communion and a sharing in common. Knowledge puffs up, too much food can make us swell up, but love and fellowship help us build each other up (see 1 Cor. 8:1). When we help another with severe burdens, we participate in fellowship.

QUESTIONS

1. Have you ever struggled with your diet?

_____

_____

_____

_____

2. What was your metabolism like when you were younger?

_____

_____

_____

_____

3. Do you find yourself struggling when it comes to an "all-you-can-eat buffet?"

_____

_____

_____

_____

4. How would you describe the correlation between food and our spiritual lives?

_____

_____

_____

_____

5. How well do we help others with their burdens?

_____

_____

_____

_____

6. How uncomfortable does it make us feel to find out about our gluttonous tendencies?

_____

_____

_____

_____

7. How often do we find forgotten leftovers which spoiled because we did not finish them?

_____

_____

_____

_____

8. How often do we help to alleviate the hunger of those who are less fortunate?

_____

_____

_____

_____

9. How often do we fast to remember those who are starving?

_____

_____

_____

_____

CHAPTER 7

THE SIN OF LUST

John 4:16-18, Matthew 5:27-28

I say unto you, that whosoever looketh on a woman to lust after her hath committed adultery with her already in his heart.

—Matt. 5:28 KJV[1]

Our addictions make us cling to what the world proclaims as the keys to self-fulfillment, which are: accumulation of wealth and power; attainment of status and admiration; lavish consumption of food and drink; and sexual gratification without distinguishing between lust and love. The addicted life can aptly be designated a life lived in "a distant country." Beneath it all is the great rebellion, the unspoken curse: "I wish you were dead."

—Henri Nouwen in The Return of the Prodigal,
Christianity Today, Vol. 36, no. 10.[2]

Lust, I read somewhere, is the craving for salt by a man who is dying of thirst.

—Name Withheld[3]

Unbridled lust:

A cannibal committing suicide
By nibbling on himself.

—Calvin Miller[4]

I've looked on a lot of women with lust. I've committed adultery in
my heart a number of times. This is something that God recognizes
I will do…and God forgives me for it.

—Jimmy Carter[5]

Lust and reason are enemies. Solomon Ben Gabirol (c. 1020–1070)[6]

Sins of the flesh are never to be reasoned or parleyed with. There
is no more reasoning with them than the winds. Understanding is
nonplused, for lust like hurricane of sand, blinds the eyes. We must
fly. It is true valor in such a case as to turn the back.[7]

JAMES 1:14 REMINDS us that "Everyone is tempted by their own
cravings; they are lured away and enticed by them" (CEB). The world
we live in today bombards us with suggestive messages in the advertising
and entertainment business. How often do we see a commercial on TV
that is loaded with racy ideas? How often do we hear suggestive lyrics in
a song on the radio? How often do we see movies (either when watching
one or looking for one to rent) that are rated R because of the sexual
content? It is almost inescapable. That's why most R-rated movies are
for mature audiences only! No matter how guarded one might be, the
barrage of racy and suggestive messages never seems to stop.

Cell phones now make it possible for inappropriate interaction
between people. Kids can now use cell phones to send lewd messages
and pictures. They call this practice of sending lewd pictures "sexting."
Once something is public on the web or over the cell phone messaging
network, it can go viral.

William Barclay shared an excellent insight about the early church. The influence of the early church changed the world because of how Christians practiced a different set of values. "Chastity was the one completely new virtue that Christianity brought into the world. In the ancient world sexual relationships before marriage and outside marriage were the normal and accepted practice. The sexual appetite was regarded as a thing to be gratified, not to be controlled. That is an attitude that is not unfamiliar today, although often it is supported by specious arguments."[8] The church needs to make herself known now, just as it did then, if we are to witness effectively in the world.

The apostle Paul gave us this warning: "See to it that no one takes you captive through hollow and deceptive philosophy, which depends on human tradition and the basic principles of this world rather than on Christ" (Colossians 2:8 NIV). The world we live in is filled with hollow and deceptive philosophy. Jesus encountered a captive person when he met the woman at the well in John 4.

Billy Graham described impurity (lust) as one of America's biggest sins.[9] Lust (impurity) bears bad fruit, and it needs a remedy.

IMPURITY IS AMERICA'S BIGGEST SIN

Lust receives great press. In his book, *The Seven Deadly Sins*, Billy Graham made the point that, "Impurity obviously has a better press agent than purity....In selling 'sex' wholesale the momentary thrill is played up, but the consequences of this vicious sin are played down."[10] It makes money for those who target lustful tendencies in human nature as a conduit for a marketing strategy. Though it may be subtle, it exploits those it uses as its subjects in such marketing strategies. It also targets an audience that has young and impressionable people. Graham also says, "Impurity is one of the most revolting sins because it twists and distorts one of God's most precious gifts to man—human love—and drags it down to the level of the beast."[11] Lust is what distorts the understanding of love as God intended it to be because lust reduces people from human to a non-human perception wherein he/she becomes an object. Lust requires no commitment, only gratification. It feeds the flesh's desire, while it leaves the soul not just hungry, but starving and thirsting for what is missing. That is the issue Jesus addressed when he ministered to the woman at the well in John 4.

Just recently on the radio, a comparison was made between two female recording artists with obviously different styles. One was Taylor Swift and the other was Lady Gaga. In a comparison of the sales of the two different magazines featuring these two artists, one was more popular than the other. Taylor Swift's clean-cut image was less popular in magazine sales than Lady Gaga's enticing look.

Impurity and immorality do not seem to come with a warning label. Years ago, the Surgeon General did what was necessary to cause tobacco companies to put warning labels on cigarette packs: "Smoking Causes Lung Cancer, Heart Disease, Emphysema, and May Complicate Pregnancy." However, it was years before that warning was placed on the boxes of cigarettes. It makes you stop and think about how many people died from the problems caused by smoking cigarettes before the problem was taken seriously enough to mandate the warning on cigarette boxes!

It was not until the late 1990s that the entertainment industry started to rate the shows we see on television. Now, at the beginning of TV shows, we can see icons that indicate what is appropriate for different age levels. The entertainment industry was already doing that with movies. So why did it take them so long to start putting ratings on TV shows and music (tapes, LPs and CDs)? A rating system should have already been mandated to the rock music industry! Tipper Gore, along with the PMRC (Parents Music Resource Center), made recommendations about those matters in 1987. They were finally put into action, but why did it take so long? [12]

Pornography is another concern. People think of pornography only as nude photos in magazines and X-rated films. However, there is more to it than that. Pornography also involves the rock music industry. Tipper Gore makes a valid point in her book, *Raising PG Kids in an X-Rated Society*. She points out a known fact that children under 17 cannot attend a movie rated R. No one under 18 can buy a *Playboy* magazine. However, minors can sometimes buy compact discs with pornographic pictures and suggestions.[13]

In his book, *The Closing of the American Mind*, Alan Bloom points out how rock music is dangerous to today's youth. According to Bloom, "Rock gives children on a silver platter, with all the public authority of the entertainment industry, everything their parents always used to tell them they had to wait for until they grew up and would understand later."[14] In other words, Bloom is saying that rock music and the entertainment industry included therein is educating our youth about "… sexual desire undeveloped and untutored"[15] prematurely whether we realize it or not. There are those who hide behind the mask of denial when it comes to this problem. Some justify their stance with the first amendment as they claim it is nothing more than an art form. But truthfully, it exploits those who buy pornographic items because someone else is getting rich from their lust. There can be no doubt that pornography feeds the sin of lust. Furthermore, pornography is degrading to women because they are usually portrayed as objects of desire rather than as people!

THE FRUIT OF IMPURITY

Lust desecrates what God intended to be holy. God created everything and made it good (see Gen. 1:31). Man thought he could improve the good thing God created by following his own agenda. In following our own agenda, we stray from the way God intended things to be.

There is a story from Greek mythology about a girl who was named Pandora. She was given a box with contents that would be harmful if she was to open the box. She was warned not to open it for this reason. But as the story goes, her curiosity got the best of her. She opened the box, and out came all of its harmful contents. Realizing what had happened, she tried to close the lid, but she was too late. However, *hope* also came out of the box. It was the only good thing in there.[16]

Adam and Eve sure made a mess of the order God created. It was because of their yielding to the temptation to know more than God wanted them to know that things got messed up (see Gen. 3). Impurity tempts us in a similar way. Like the "forbidden fruit," it looks beautiful and attractive. Yet, it is forbidden for a reason. The reason is that once we yield to the temptation, we lose something of our innocence.

It's true that we reap what we sow (see Gal. 6:7). There is an old saying, "Sow an act and reap a habit; sow a habit and reap a character; sow a character and reap a destiny."[17] Like all other sin, impurity looks promising and entertaining at first. In the end, yielding to its immoral temptations does nothing more than reward us with pain, guilt, and unwanted consequences. In some cases, the consequences may be remorse. In other cases, the result may be a disease. One of the diseases that comes from such a lifestyle is HIV, which leads to AIDS. Still in other cases, the result may be an unwanted pregnancy—the result of pre-marital sex or an affair.

At first, sin might make us feel guilty. As Barclay notes, sin kills innocence, ideals and the will.[18] The reason it becomes easier to sin is because we become anesthetized (numb) to guilt. When the fruit of the sin of immorality reaches its end, it is then possible for people to see that what they reaped was something they wished they had never sown.

Billy Graham outlines how lust and impurity work. "First, the sin of impurity marks. In the days of slavery a slave could be identified by his master. Next, impurity mocks or deceives." The last point that Billy Graham makes about the fact of impurity is that "when it is finished, it brings forth remorse."[19] Billy Graham echoes James 1:14 -15. "Everyone is tempted by their own cravings; they are lured away and enticed by them. Once those cravings conceive, they give birth to sin; and when sin grows up, it gives birth to death" (CEB).

There is no question that God forgives penitent sinners. As 1 John 1:9 says, "But if we confess our sins, he is faithful and just to forgive us our sins and cleanse us from everything we've done wrong" (CEB). Even though God forgives us of our sins when we ask Him, the consequences of that sinful lifestyle are something that may remain. Think about these consequences of immoral behavior: unwanted pregnancies and sexually transmitted diseases. What about girls who have gotten pregnant out of wedlock and have sacrificed their future to raise those children themselves, or the guilt they suffered from having to put their children up for adoption because they could not take care of them?

In college, I took a public speaking course where one of the assignments was to take a stand on an issue and argue for it in a debate. Next, your opponent would state his case. It seemed to resemble a courtroom where two lawyers oppose one another. I was given the assignment to argue against abortion while my opponent was to argue for it. The debate took place. He won...I lost. It seems that people did not feel that an unborn child was considered a person in the timeframe that an abortion could be done (the first trimester). I talked with one of my fellow classmates after class. He said he had gotten his girlfriend an abortion back in high school. He said he was glad he had. He said that if he hadn't done it, it would have messed up both of their lives. The whole time, I kept thinking about the life of the child that they had overlooked. Years later, he is now probably married and has children. I wonder how he feels every time he sees a child. I would not want to even imagine what a burden that kind of guilt would be.

THE REMEDY FOR IMPURITY

Prayer is one way we can keep our focus on God. It has been said that "prayer will keep us from sin or sin will keep us from prayer." Like the hymn, "Stand Up, Stand Up for Jesus" says in the third stanza, "stand in his strength alone; the arm of flesh will fail you, ye dare not trust your own. Put on the gospel armor, each piece put on with prayer; where duty calls or danger, be never wanting there."[20] Obviously, this stanza is referring to Ephesians 6:10-20.

Jesus told us to avoid compromising our faith. He said that if our right eye offends us, we should cut it out and throw it away. It is better to lose one part of our body than for our whole body to be thrown into hell. He said the same about the hand (see Matt. 5: 27-30). In that passage of scripture, Jesus did not mean for us to literally cut off our limbs and pluck out our eyes. No, what He meant was for us not to put ourselves in a situation where we would tempt ourselves, compromise our faith and values, and succumb to sinful behavior. Therefore, if something causes us to sin, we should cut that temptation out of our lives so that we master it rather than letting it master us.

Everyone hungers for the feeling of being important to others. We all want a life that matters. It was true for the woman at the well in John 4, and it's true for us. Lust is no substitute for love. It is certainly no substitute for our Lord, who should have first place in our lives. Jesus helped the woman at the well see that drinking from the supernatural water He gave her would satisfy her spiritual hunger and thirst because it would become a spring of water that bubbles up unto eternal life (see John 4:13-14 CEB).

Matthew 5:8 says, "Blessed are the pure in heart, for they shall see God." The woman at the well was beginning to see Jesus as her heart was becoming pure. Impurity blinds our eyes to God's glory. I close with the words of the apostle Paul. "Whatever is true, whatever is noble, whatever is right, whatever is pure, whatever is lovely, whatever is admirable—if anything is excellent or praiseworthy—think about such things" (Philippians 4:8 NIV).

QUESTIONS

1. How do you see lust as a problem in our country?

   _____

   _____

   _____

   _____

2. How do you see lust displayed in our American culture?

   _____

   _____

   _____

   _____

3. How do you see lust displayed in our culture now compared to 50 years ago? One hundred years ago?

   _____

   _____

   _____

   _____

4. Is it possible for lust to start out as a subtle thing that winds up becoming an enslaving thing?

   _____

   _____

_____

_____

5. How do you feel about the contrast between Taylor Swift and Lady Gaga?

_____

_____

_____

_____

6. How do you feel about Alan Bloom's conclusion that youth are exposed to things that they are not always mature enough to handle?

_____

_____

_____

_____

7. How do you think our country compares with other countries when it comes to lust?

_____

_____

_____

_____

8. How has lust affected you?

_____

_____

_____

_____

9. How can the church of today help to change the world as the early church did?

_____

_____

_____

_____

WORKS CITED

Chapter 1

1. Vernon McClellan. *Timeless Treasures*. Peabody: Hendrickson Publishers, Inc. 2000.
2. Ibid.
3. R. Daniel Watkins. *Encyclopedia of Compelling Quotations*. Peabody: Hendrickson Publishers, Inc. 2001.
4. Ibid.
5. Ibid.
6. Ibid.
7. Ibid.
8. Ibid.
9. Ibid.
10. Ibid.
11. Ernest A. Fitzgerald. *Keeping Pace: Inspirations in the Air*. Greensboro: Pace Communications Inc., 1988, p. 210.
12. James S. Hewett. ed. *Illustrations Unlimited*. Wheaton: Tyndale House Publishers, Inc., 1988, p. 295.
13. Fred B. Craddock. *Interpretation: A Bible Commentary for Teaching and Preaching: Luke*. Louisville John Knox Press, 1990, p. 211.

14. Billy Graham. *The 7 Deadly Sins*. Grand Rapids: Zondervan Publishing House, 1955, p. 17.
15. George A. Buttrick. ed. *The Interpreter's Bible*. Volume 7. Nashville: Abingdon Press, 1988, p. 310).
16. William P. Barkers. ed. *Tarbell's Teacher's Guide*. 86th Annual Volume. Elgin: David C. Cook Publishing Co. 1989, p. 97.

Chapter 2

1. Elisha Hodge. *Today's Best Illustrations*. Volumes 1-4 *Christianity Today*, Inc, 1997, Electronic Edition STEP Files Copyright © 2005, QuickVerse.
2. Robert Shannon. *1000 Windows: A Speaker's Sourcebook of Illustrations*. Cincinnati: The Standard Publishing Co, 1997. Electronic Edition Step Files, QuickVerse, 2005.
3. Bob Phillips. *Philipps Book of Greta Thoughts and Sayings*. Tyndale House Publishers, Inc. 1993. Electronic Edition Step Files, QuickVerse, 2005.
4. Ibid.
5. Ibid.
6. Ibid.
7. Vern McClellan and Croft M. Pentz. *The Complete Book of Proverbs, Wacky Wit and Zingers*. Zingers 1990, Wacky Wit, 1996. Wheaton: Tyndale House Publishers, Inc. Electronic Edition Step Files, QuickVerse, 2005.
8. Elesha Hodge. *Today's Best Illustrations*, Volumes 1–4. Christianity Today, Inc. 1997. Electronic Edition Step Files, QuickVerse, 2005.
9. Billy Graham. *The 7 Deadly Sins*. Grand Rapids: Zondervan Publishing House, 1955, pp. 41–42
10. Ibid.
11. William R. White. *Fatal Attractions: Sermons on the Seven Deadly Sins*. Nashville: Abingdon Press, 1992, p. 30.

12. Ibid.
13. George A. Buttrick. ed. *The Interpreter's Bible.* Volume 7. Halford E. Luccock. "The Gospel According to St. Mark: Exposition." Nashville: Abingdon Press, 1988, p 753.
14. Ibid. p. 753.
15. William R. White. *Fatal Attractions: Sermons on the Seven Deadly Sins.* p. 30.
16. Edith Hamilton. *Mythology.* New York: Mentor, 1969, pp. 87-88.
17. Raymond McHenry. ed. *McHenry's Quips, Quotes and Other Notes.* [quoted from: Doyle L. Young. *New Life for Your Church,* 1989, p. 63]. Third Printing. Peabody: Hendrickson Publishers, 2004, p. 270.
18. Herb Miller. *Actions Speak Louder Than Verbs.* Nashville: Abingdon Press, 1989, p. 121.
19. William R. White. *Fatal Attractions: Sermons on the Seven Deadly Sins.* p. 30.
20. George A. Buttrick, ed. *The Interpreter's Dictionary of the Bible.* Volume A-D. Elizabeth R. Achtemeier. "Covetousness." Nashville: Abingdon Press, 1989, p. 724.
21. William R. White. *Fatal Attractions: Sermons on the Seven Deadly Sins.* p. 31.
22. Billy Graham. *The 7 Deadly Sins.* pp. 50 -51.

Chapter 3

1. Raymond McHenry. ed. *McHenry's Quips, Quotes and Other Notes.* Third Printing. Peabody: Hendrickson Publishers, 2004.
2. The Holy Bible. King James Version.
3. Ibid.
4. Ibid.
5. R. Daniel Watkins. *Encyclopedia of Compelling Quotations.* Peabody: Hendrickson Publishers, Inc. 2001.
6. Ibid.

7. Ibid.

8. Ibid.

9. Ibid.

10. Gary Smalley. *Love Is a Decision*. Dallas: Word Publishing, 1989, p. 78.

11. Theodore W. Engstrom. *227 Heart Warming Illustrations*. Grand Rapids: Zondervan Publishing House, 1953, p. 37.

12. Ibid.

13. William Barclay. *The Daily Study Bible Study: The Gospel of Matthew.* Volume 1. Revised Edition. Philadelphia: Westminster Press, 1975, pp. 327 – 328.

14. William Barclay, p. 138.

15. William Barclay, p. 138.

16. John Wesley's Notes on the Whole Bible.

17. William Barclay, p. 139.

18. Gary Smalley. *Love Is a Decision*, pp. 81-92.

19. Ibid, p. 81.

Chapter 4

1. R. Daniel Watkins. *Encyclopedia of Compelling Quotations*. Peabody: Hendrickson Publishers, Inc. 2001.

2. Ibid.

3. Ibid.

4. Ibid.

5. R. Daniel Watkins. *Encyclopedia of Compelling Quotations*. Peabody: Hendrickson Publishers, Inc. 2001.

6. Ibid.

7. Bob Phillips. *Phillips Book of Great Thoughts and Sayings*. Tyndale House Publishers, Inc. 1993. Electronic Edition Step Files, QuickVerse, 2005.

8. Ibid.

9. Ibid.

10. *Today's Best Illustrations*, Volume 5. Bible Illustrator annual supplements from 1998-2001. Electronic Edition Step Files, QuickVerse, 2005.

11. Ibid.

12. Billy Graham. *The 7 Deadly Sins*. Grand Rapids: Zondervan Publishing House, 1955, p. 88.

13. William R. White. *Fatal Attractions: Sermons on the Seven Deadly Sins*. Nashville: Abingdon Press, 1992, p. 43.

14. Warren Wiersbe, *The Bible Exposition Commentary*. Volume 1. Wheaton: Victor Books, 1989, p. 355.

15. Max Lucado. *No Wonder They Call Him Savior*. Multnomah Press, 1986, p. 125.

16. William P. Barker, ed. *Tarbell's Teacher's Guide*. 86th Annual Volume. September 1990 - August 1991. Elgin: David C. Cook Publishing Co. 1990, pp. 157-158.

Chapter 5

1. Raymond McHenry. ed. *McHenry's Quips, Quotes and Other Notes.* [quoted from: Doyle L. Young. *New Life for Your Church*, 1989, p. 63]. Third Printing. Peabody: Hendrickson Publishers, 2004.

2. Elesha Hodge. *Today's Best Illustrations*. Volumes 1-4. Christianity Today, Inc. 1997. Electronic Edition Step Files, QuickVerse, 2005.

3. Ruth Peters. Compiler. *Illustrations of Bible Truths*. AMG International, 1995. Electronic Edition Step Files, QuickVerse, 2005.

4. Robert Shannon. *1000 Windows: A Speaker's Sourcebook of Illustrations*. Cincinnati: The Standard Publishing Co, 1997. Electronic Edition Step Files, QuickVerse, 2005.

5. Ibid.

6. Ibid.

7. *Draper's Book of Quotations for the Christian World.* Edythe Draper Tyndale House Publishers, Inc. Wheaton, Illinois.
8. James M. Efird. *The New Testament Writings.* Atlanta: John Knox Press, 1980, p. 128.
9. Billy Graham. *The 7 Deadly Sins.* p. 107.
10. Ernest A. Fitzgerald. *Keeping Pace: Inspirations in the Air.* Greensboro: Pace Communications Inc., p. 161.
11. Ibid. p. 162.
12. Ibid. p. 162.
13. Geoffrey Chaucer's *The Canterbury Tales* "The Pardoner's Tale." (1340? - 1400).

Chapter 6

1. The Holy Bible. The New Revised Standard Version.
2. Bob Phillips. *Phillips Book of Great Thoughts and Sayings.* Tyndale House Publishers, Inc. 1993. Electronic Edition Step Files, Quick Verse, 2005.
3. R. Daniel Watkins. *Encyclopedia of Compelling Quotations.* Peabody: Hendrickson Publishers, Inc. 2001
4. Ibid.
5. Ibid.
6. Ibid.
7. Ibid.
8. Ibid.
9. Raymond McHenry. ed. *McHenry's Quips, Quotes and Other Notes.* Third Printing. Peabody: Hendrickson Publishers, 2004.
10. Elesha Hodge. *Today's Best Illustrations.* Volumes 1 – 4. Christianity Today, Inc. 1997. Electronic Edition Step Files, QuickVerse, 2005.
11. The Holy Bible. King James Version.
12. Ibid.

13. William R. White. *Fatal Attractions: Sermons on the Seven Deadly Sins*. Nashville: Abingdon Press, 1992, p. 56.
14. *Independent Mail* (Newspaper in Anderson, South Carolina: date of newspaper clipping not known).
15. Richard Bach. *Jonathon Livingston Seagull*. Avon: New York, 1970.

Chapter 7

1. The Holy Bible. King James Version.
2. Elesha Hodge. *Today's Best Illustrations*. Volumes 1-4. Christianity Today, Inc. 1997. Electronic Edition Step Files, QuickVerse, 2005.
3. Ibid.
4. Ibid.
5. R. Daniel Watkins. *Encyclopedia of Compelling Quotations*. Peabody: Hendrickson Publishers, Inc. 2001.
6. *Draper's Book of Quotations for the Christian World*. Edythe Draper. Tyndale House Publishers, Inc. Wheaton, Illinois.
7. Tom Carter. compiler. *Spurgeon at His Best*. Grand Rapids: Baker Book House, 1988, p. 349.
8. William Barclay. *The Daily Study Bible Series: The Letters to the Philipians, Colossians and Thessalonians*. Revised Edition. Louisville: Westminster Press, 1975, pp. 150-151.
9. Billy Graham. *The 7 Deadly Sins*. Grand Rapids: Zondervan Publishing House, 1955.
10. Ibid, p. 56.
11. Ibid, p. 56.
12. Tipper Gore. *Raising PG Kids in an X-Rated Society*. Nashville: Abingdon Press, 1987, p. 30.
13. Ibid, p. 28.
14. Alan Bloom. *The Closing of the American Mind*. New York: Simon and Schuster, 1987, p. 73.
15. Ibid, p. 73.

16. Edith Hamilton. *Mythology*. New York: Mentor Books, 1942, pp. 70 -72.

17. William Barclay. *The Daily Study Bible Series. The Letters to the Galatians and the Ephesians*. Revised Edition. Philadelphia: Westminster Press, 1975, pp. 97-98.

18. Ibid, pp. 97-99.

19. Billy Graham. *The 7 Deadly Sins*, p. 59.

20. *The United Methodist Hymnal*. Nashville: The United Methodist Publishing House, 1989, p. 514.

To order additional copies of this book,
please visit www.redemption-press.com
Also available on Amazon.com and BarnesandNoble.com
Or by calling toll free 1+ (844) 273-3336

CPSIA information can be obtained
at www.ICGtesting.com
Printed in the USA
LVHW081032210223
740044LV00012B/348